The Beatles' Ten

Commandments

Joshua Reeves

Commandment 1- Can't Buy Me Love

Commandment 2- Think For Yourself

Commandment 3- Tomorrow Never Knows

Commandment 4- Nothing is Real and Nothing to
Get Hung About

Commandment 5- All You Need is Love

Commandment 6- Don't You Know it's Gonna be
Alright

Commandment 7- Ob-la-Di Ob-la-Da Life Goes On

Commandment 8- Come Together

Commandment 9- Let it Be

Commandment 10- And in the End the Love You
Take is Equal to the Love You Make

Music as Spirituality

Jeff Tweedy, lead singer of the band Wilco, sings on the nineties indie anthem "Sunken Treasure" that music is his savior.

Looking back on my first recollection of something infinite, I think back to my father's record collection. Dad had crates of records that seemed to be never ending. Not just records, but in between each groove another story. These records were symbolic of what the spiritual life might actually be. Our experiences were perhaps, not one and done, but something that could be played over, and each time, if you listened carefully, often with more wisdom than before, couldn't you hear something brand new?

The songs on an album didn't teach statistical information, like the subjects in school. They sounded like they could be about me, and prepared me for wisdom. I learned about what romance was like, what loss was like, what standing up for what you believe in is like, and what it's like to feel cool. In my life, music was the best medium to prepare me for those experiences.

In his "Song of Myself," Walt Whitman speaks of the child who pulls a handful of grass from the ground. The speaker asks the child what he is holding. Whitman admits to himself that he knows no more than the boy might. The grass is a metaphor for life; it cannot be fully known or explained, it must be experienced. Just like a record, you can't show it to Dad and ask him what it is; he has to play it for you, and you yourself must come to know the music.

At the heart of Dad's collection were his Beatles records, which alone seemed never-ending—The U.K. and U.S. versions, the bootlegs and 45's, and the solo stuff too. These were the most praised and revered.

Music became a sort of spirituality for me because it was expansive and to fully grasp it required devotion. It expressed love, hope, fear, included birth and death, and repeated listenings offered the opportunity to be inducted into life's most important undertakings. When participated in with equanimity, music is not unlike a religious ritual; transformational and putting one into contact with what is most sacred in life.

John Lennon got in trouble for saying that the Beatles were more popular than Jesus, but was he wrong? No offense to Jesus, but could Lennon's comment be a statement that rock and roll was starting to overtake religion as the central way in which people were sorting out the questions of life, morality, and love?

Influence

Question: who has had the most significant spiritual impact in the last hundred years?

Is it an institution like the Catholic Church or the Latter Day Saints? Even with rapid population growth, religious affiliation seems to have declined, especially in the latter part of the last century.

Perhaps it is the message of unity and non-violence, as practiced vigilantly by Gandhi and King? These movements have certainly affected social structures and individual liberties, but at the same time, the pacifism underlying their views has certainly not struck the social match to light those who need it most.

How about Science Fiction? *Star Wars*, *Star Trek*, even "fantasy" works like *Harry*

Potter? Certainly the sense of adventure and wisdom espoused in these tales has been monumental. In an era where information is so accessible, people are certainly more familiar with the characters in *Star Wars* than characters in the Bible or with the Buddha's noble truths.

These answers are all easy to argue for, not only for their positive impact, but their negative impact as well.

I would argue the music of the Beatles has had a greater spiritual and cultural impact on peoples of the world than any individual or medium.

The Beatles have sold over a billion albums. Many radio stations not only play the Beatles regularly, but some even have Sunday morning rituals (sound familiar?) honoring them.

Mikhail Gorbechev, the last leader of the U.S.S.R. said: "more than any ideology, more than any religion, more than Vietnam or any war or nuclear bomb, the single most important reason for the diffusion of the Cold War was...the Beatles."

The Beatles might have been the foremost power in the westernization of the world, championing a message of independence, love, and personal liberation.

The Beatles' message should be taken quite seriously. This is not to call this book serious; however, the message of the Beatles is worth focusing on. The Beatles share a unique wisdom, influenced by many sources that, if applied to our lives, have serious spiritual and practical consequences.

The Beatles' Ten Commandments is not meant to be a work of fiction or non-fiction—it is an interpretation of the Beatles work, symbolism, and legend explored through a context of spiritual wisdom as opposed to pop-culture.

The Songs

"After silence that which comes nearest to expressing the inexpressible is music."

-Aldous Huxley

Music has too often been dismissed as an obscurity with little value for wisdom by those who prefer the generally considered more boring mediums of lecturing, professing and pestilent preaching.

Schopenhauer put it in a more elegant and complicated way:

"This art is *music*. It stands quite apart from all the others. In it we do not recognize the copy, the repetition, of any idea of the inner nature of the world. Yet it is such a great and exceedingly fine art, its effect on man's innermost nature is so powerful, and it is so completely and profoundly understood by him in his innermost being as an entirely universal language, whose distinctness surpasses even that of the world of perception itself, that in it we certainly have to look for more than that 'exercise in arithmetic in which the mind does not know it is counting.'"

There's something about music that "speaks" to many of us like no other medium. It carries enchanted mysteries as well as memories of our life narratives, hopes and fears. Music teaches us to love, to mourn, to hope, and to let go.

Have you ever experienced the phenomenon of feeling like a song was exactly about you? Music, like the greatest stories, resonates in us as we find our place in it.

Music is a source of meaning and wisdom. This is not a new understanding. Historians believe the oldest expressions in the Bible are contained in the book entitled "Psalms," which means "Songs." These "Songs" come long before the written word, and like any good song, could easily be retained in memory and conveyed to others.

I know people who can reread the same book or watch the same movie over and over again, but I'd argue that nothing is a more preferable re-experience than a good song. A good tune has a way of retrieving our capacity to hear, not just at a sense level, but a level of heart and soul.

Then there is that phenomenon of "getting sick" of something. This can happen to anything repeated to the point of near perversity, including music.

You listen to the same song again and over; let's say it is Van Morrison's "Brown Eyed Girl." After a while you're "sick of it." You are sure you know every harmony and lyric.

Several years later you hear "Brown Eyed Girl" and it sounds brand new, like when you heard it for the first time. Here is a lovely phenomenon, getting "well with something." You realize when you were sick of the song, it wasn't the song, but your experience of it that was making you ill.

How easy it is to forget to "Dance to the Music."

"The Fab Four"

Paul, John, George, and Ringo became known as "The Fab Four." It is not the purpose of this book to be biographical or chronological, but metaphorical. Who "The Fab Four" were as men is the trust and pleasure of an ever receding collection of individuals. I'm more interested in the ensuing legends.

Each Beatle has a unique voice and message for us to identify with.

Paul- Evolving Love

Paul's story in the Beatles is one of an ever evolving understanding of life and love. It is through love and loving that Paul comes to his understanding of the Divine and his relationship to it.

Paul's initial understanding of love is well represented in the song "Yesterday." In the song, love for Paul is something not present, but clearly "Yesterday," and past. It is a game he played, and as the lyrics suggest, one he's lost. It is not something he is, but something to be won and provided to him by something else, preferably gorgeous.

Paul's next evolution in love is well symbolized in the song "I've Just Seen a Face." Love becomes something not of the past, but a mysterious and powerful presence that strikes

Paul in the present. Listening to the song Paul's transition from "Yesterday" makes it clear that had it been another day (yesterday, for example) he would have looked away.

In order for Paul to grow in love, he had to stop looking the other way, yesterday, and come present and "open." Love is still something that is not seen as his own, but must come to him, still from a female.

Paul makes a large leap from "I've Just Seen a Face" to "Here, There, and Everywhere." Although the lyrics seem directed at the feminine, she is no longer just a body, but a presence. Love is no longer a form to find or be found by, but a presence that is always there. Paul realizes that to live life to the fullest, love cannot be in the past, nor even be promised in the future, it must be here.

Finally for Paul love takes the shape of the Divine Mother, in "Let it Be." The Divine

Mother is one of the most sacred and powerful symbols in spirituality, representing unconditional love. She whispers words of wisdom to him, loving him always.

John- Individuation

John's evolution through the Beatles is one of what the wise Carl Jung termed "individuation." It is the wholeness of an individual coming about through the uniting of opposite aspects in the personality.

Where Paul's path is easy to explain in songs, John is better viewed through albums. John's legend today is already well developed as a prophet of peace and love for all. John, however, had another and very important side. A "shadow side" as Jung would put it.

There is no doubt that as the Beatles' music evolved, so did the "Fab Four" as individuals. Central to this was their own spiritual search. For John, this is symbolized through an inner journey of simultaneously being a wise man and a lost boy. On *Beatles for Sale*, he is a "Loser" who wants to love you "Eight Days a Week."

On "Help," the message is self-explanatory, but he is willing to show his more stable face in "Tell me What You See,"; however, the question of who he really is ends up being left to the subject of the song. At some level, the subject is himself.

Things get a little awkward on *Rubber Soul* when "In My Life" is grooves away from "Run for Your Life"; then on the White Album, one moment Lennon is telling us that everything is going to be alright, then he is crooning that he is lonely and wants to die.

John's individuation does take place, through exploring images and creative themes. They make little sense to the listener, but they contain a rhythm that facilitates John's exploration of light and dark, as well as his own authenticity. As the lyrics reveal, he eventually "comes together."

George- Finding your own voice

The following statement from George Harrison says much about his musical journey:

"I remember thinking I just want more. This isn't it. Fame is not the goal. Money is not the goal. To be able to know how to get peace of mind, how to be happy, is something you don't just stumble across. You've got to search for it."

George's evolution is a hero's tale on finding your own voice. Certainly, George didn't have immense illusions about John and Paul, but we sure do, and thus we can be awestruck at how the best of George comes forth.

When he writes a song that is capable of standing up with the others on an album, and then another, and then is featured on a single, it is an impressive feat.

George finds his voice by loving God. By loving God he creates some of the most beautiful songs including "Something." Harrison teaches us that the best way to sing a love song is to direct it toward the divine.

Of course, we can find our true voice with the help of our friends, but eventually we must use it ourselves. It is of no coincidence that George's masterpiece, "My Sweet Lord," comes when he goes solo. Yet, as his words reveal, perhaps he never quite felt he really left?

"Most people's reality is an illusion, a great big illusion. You automatically have to succumb to the illusion that 'I am this body'. I am not George. I am not really George. I am this living thing that goes on, always has been, always will be, but at this time I happen to be in 'this' body. The body has changed; was a baby, was a young man, will soon be an old man, and I'll be dead. The physical body will pass but this bit in the

middle,

that's the only reality. All the rest is the

illusion,

so to say that somebody thinks we are, the

ex-

Beatles are removed from reality in their

personal concept. It does not have any truth

to it just because somebody thinks it. They

are the concepts which become layer upon

layer of illusion. Why live in the darkness

all your life? Why, if you are unhappy, if

you are having a miserable time, why not just

look at it. Why are you in the darkness? Look

for the light. The light is within. That is

the big message."

Ringo- The "Every Man"

In the Beatles, Ringo is the everyman. He is in a sense all of us along for the ride. He symbolizes steadiness, contentedness, and a clear witness as transformation takes place. What else is "With a Little Help from My Friends" but a witnessing to his band mates as he sings about the importance of togetherness?

It is unwise to underappreciate Ringo's importance to the Beatles. One could argue, "It could be anybody," but when you think about it, how rare and unique is the "everyman?" Ringo is willing to play along, without causing any trouble:

> "I've never been able to sit round on my own and play drums, practice in the back room, never been able to. I've always played with other musicians. It's how I play, there's no joy for me in playing on my own, bashing

away. I need a bass, a piano, guitar, whatever, and then I can play."

In order to have an honest approach to spirituality through the Beatles work, we must not only hear ourselves in them, but them in ourselves. The Beatles connect us with the parts of ourselves, learning to love, learning to be whole, learning to find our voice, and learning to be consistent and true.

The Beatles' First Commandment

"Can't Buy Me Love"

The Beatles first commandment is a warning against spiritual materialism.

It's a proverb that reminds us that no thing can encase that which is more valuable than its form.

If you're like me, you might like to think, from time to time, "I'm a real love-machine." Truth be told, we are all just vehicles for love and hopefully faithful stewards of it for a time.

Love is hopefully an affect for all of us, but it is bigger than all of us too. The musician Frank Black sang in one of his songs "Sad Old World" that he doesn't know anyone who doesn't try to give it a whirl.

If you walk into a convenience store you may find as you peruse through the soft drinks many will be labeled with spiritual qualities like "energy and relaxation." SOBE even put out a drink called "Nirvana." This is an example of spiritual materialism- the belief that an object is the quality itself. Spiritual materialism is normally accompanied with the belief that the quality we seek is not already readily available within ourselves. When it comes to a soft drink, it may not matter much. But when it comes to the objects of our affection, to those we look up to, or images of ourselves we may never become, we can so far separate the spiritual qualities we long to feel so far from ourselves; they become permanently "other" than who we are.

If in a relationship, you are my love, what happens when you go for a walk? My love is absent. What happens if you leave me? My love is gone. Either I must find someone else to take your place, or come to realize that love was not mine to give or take in the first place. It is not for sale.

Just because the Beatles didn't "care too much for money" certainly doesn't mean they lacked it. The Beatles are a great story about capitalism in action, and they deserved all that they got. Since love is the priority, money isn't significant, but can something buy you love? It's about as odd a question spiritually as asking what buys money might be practically. Money doesn't get purchased; it spends, it purchases, it invests, and it returns. So it is with love. Ideally it reciprocates and grows and "interests." But if you see a beautiful woman, don't try to purchase her and don't try to spend her either. Just use the currency in your own heart, invest wisely, and hopefully it will return.

The Beatles' Second Commandment

"Think for Yourself"

The Beatles second commandment is a warning against not utilizing our own minds.

"Think for Yourself" might be the most spiritually radical of the Beatles' ten commandments. How many Sunday morning pulpits will involve a pastor saying something like, "my message today is think for yourself?" Not many, if any at all. In religion and in any philosophy that seeks answers beyond one's own use of their minds, thinking, and critical thinking in particular is frowned upon.

The profound thinker Alan Watts used to point out a simple fact of life- you can't think outside of your own mind. Our minds are vital to our experience of life and they are not what stands between what is true and ourselves, but the only chance that they might be connected in a way that we can grasp. Life certainly is what it is whether we know it or not, but could we say that if our own minds are the only vessel for our understanding of life, we get the life that we deserve?

The song itself would be quite interesting if God sung it to Moses through the burning bush, telling Moses to think for himself because he won't be there for him. Would we see this as God's great abandonment or perhaps her greatest gift?

In an age where politicians stand more for symbols than what symbols stand for and where religions tend to act less as sanctuaries and more like political parties to affiliate with, "Think For Yourself" isn't just a radical message but the most needed in our societies.

When someone tells me they don't know what they believe about life's big questions, it's hard for me to believe them. Life has a way of forcing us to believe something about whether there is a God, or if our consciousness survives our body's death...whether we know it or not, it seems to be there like a default mechanism. Those default beliefs, conscious or subjective, show up in how we live each day, in how we think of ourselves, in how we treat others.

For example, a woman may choose to leave a church because she finds its teachings overly judgmental and restrictive. What then does she believe? If she isn't sure, all she is left with is the foundation in place. Until she forms a new belief, she may have left the church, but not the judgment.

The best beliefs are never revealed, they are resolved. There is nothing wrong with taking an idea as true on faith, but there is something wrong if we do not embody it in practice. If it doesn't prove itself to us in how we live, we cease living so well. Why not think for ourselves? Is the idea of a changed

mind that scary?

The Beatles' Third Commandment

"Tomorrow Never Knows"

The Beatles/ third commandment is a warning against letting common sense keep you from the present truth.

"Tomorrow Never Knows" is a malapropism that Ringo Starr came up with which was probably a play off the phrase, "tomorrow only knows." Also, known as "Ringoisms" are "Hard Days Night" and "Eight Days a Week." They speak to the fun of seeing what wisdom we can come up with by using incorrect words where the so called "correct" ones should be. In the Beatles third commandment we receive not only a message of wisdom, but a vehicle for getting to it—a challenge to common sense.

The Beatles third commandment certainly challenges common thinking particularly the ideas that- "Only time can tell," "All in Good time," and "Good things come to those who wait."

Perhaps the Beatles meant something like what Clash front man Joe Strummer meant as quoted in the biopic *The Future is Unwritten*?

"And so now I'd like to say - people can change anything they want to. And that means everything in the world. People are running about following their little tracks - I am one of them. But we've all got to stop just following our own little mouse trail. People can do anything - this is something that I'm beginning to learn. People are out there doing bad things to each other. That's because they've been dehumanized. It's time to take the humanity back into the center of the ring and follow that for a time. Greed, it ain't going anywhere. They should have that in a big billboard across Times Square. Without people you're nothing. That's my spiel."

Play existence to the end of the beginning, The Beatles tell us. How might we interpret that? One way is to say that we can change the direction of our history, it is up to us. Another is to say the story is right here. Here is where the action is. Stop putting off your full experience of it for later.

The song "Tomorrow Never Knows" famously marks the Beatles' first notable trip into psychedelia. The psychedelic movement—minus the drugs, of course—was about new ways to live in the present. Expanding the "doors of perception" and, as noted in a previous commandment, "change your mind."

Tomorrow never knows. Why? Because knowledge only exists here and what's the most important knowledge for our lives? Our own.

The new wave band The Waitresses debut album was entitled *Wasn't Tomorrow Wonderful?* It's a fine reminder that no matter how real tomorrow may be, our experience can never arrive anywhere but here.

The Beatles Fourth Commandment

"Nothing is Real and Nothing to Get Hung About"

The Beatles Fourth Commandment is a warning against taking things too seriously.

The Beatles fourth commandment comes to us from the song "Strawberry Fields Forever." The song is an ode to the visions that accompany the changing of one's mind via psychedelics or otherwise. "Nothing is real and nothing to get hung about" is a complex commandment. First, it recalls the theory of idealism, the ancient religious Hindu idea that the material universe is but the emanation of the mind of God. Within this thought, the best metaphor for life is dream and everything is fundamentally mental.

One way to take this is, "Don't worry what happens, we'll all wake up at some point and have a big laugh about all of this."

The comedian Bill Hicks used to put it this way.

"The world is like a ride in an amusement park and when you choose to go on it you think it's real because that's how powerful our minds are. And the ride goes up and down and around and around and it has thrills and chills and it's very brightly colored and it's very loud. And it's fun - for a while. Some people have been on the ride for a long time, and they begin to question; is this real? Or is this just a ride? And other people have remembered, and they come back to us, and they say, "Hey, don't worry, don't be afraid, ever, because... this is just a ride."

Another way is to take the illusion inherent in life as a message to pay attention to a singular reality, call it Brahman (as they do in Hinduism); or God, or Holy Spirit, or just call it "Life." Pay attention to how life shows up in many forms and in many ways. Don't get hung up on it so much that you forget it is all a singular reality.

If your boyfriend breaks up with you, it's ok; don't get hung up on it because life doesn't stop. If you're not the person you want to be or living the life you want, keep living.

Perhaps "nothing is real and nothing to get hung about" is a statement we can take not as pointing to the illusions of reality, but at the truest of all realities?

We should honor the truth of our own experience, but we should also honor it enough to keep moving forward. The Beatles' fourth commandment teaches us that there is a singular reality we must be willing to let go of "illusions" to truly experience.

What illusions must the devotee let go of in order to see God? What judgments must the lover release to become enchanted? What answer must the scientist be willing to depart from to discover the truth? As Ralph Waldo Emerson argued, we must release our trust from social conventions and trust ourselves.

"To believe your own thought, to believe what is true for you in your private heart is true for all men,-that is genius."

We never have to grab onto anything to find out what is truly real; we only have to let go.

The Beatles' Fifth Commandment

"All You Need is Love"

The Beatles' fifth commandment is a warning not
to forget who we really are.

The Beatles' fifth commandment speaks to
the heart of who we are. Who are we really?
If the statement "all you need is love," is
true, we are beings that exist because of and
for love.

This is not an easy premise to accept when
you think in terms of something like Abraham
Maslow's hierarchy of needs. I need food. I
need security. Even John Lennon sings, "I need
money." Yet, even the hierarchy of needs tells
us when our most basic needs are met- we
fulfill the need of self-actualization. We
become our potential.

And it can of course be argued that the need for love is a vital need no matter what the human suffering. What becomes of a child who is unloved? What happens to a relationship where love seeks to be cultivated? What happens to our feeling of aliveness when there is no love in our hearts?

Do you remember Rudolph the Red Nose Reindeer's Christmas special—the clay-mation one from the 1960s? Rudolph and friends find themselves on the Island of Misfit Toys with the spotted elephant and the Jack in the Box named Charlie. They meet King Moon Raiser, who asks Rudolph when he gets back to Christmas town to tell Santa about the orphaned toys: a Toy is not truly real, until it is loved by a child. There is a great human truth in that idea; we are not truly real until we are loved.

The Beatles' fifth commandment points to the higher aspects of our being and calls us to pay more attention to those aspects.

In speaking to the state of American politics, Noam Chomsky famously said, "If you're not outraged, you're not paying attention." Well, we can take a spiritual perspective on that. If your heart is not in alignment with the love of your life, you're not paying attention. If tears do not well up in your eyes in awareness of all those you love and whom love you in return, you're not paying attention. If you're not in awe at the miracle of life and even more so at the realization that you are a part of that life, you're not paying attention.

From the highest of perspectives, love is all you need.

People often approach the song "All you Need is Love" with such joy that they forget the song itself has a pessimistic slant. It tells us that there is nothing that we can do that cannot be done; depending on how you listen to it, could tell us that there is nothing new that we can do, but learn to play the game, of course.

This is reminiscent of Ecclesiastes in the Hebrew Scriptures, who proclaims there's nothing new under the sun, yet "The Teacher" in Ecclesiastes does believe there is newness in life, an energy we bring to it. Perhaps this is the love we need?

There are many types of love. We need all of them, be it sweet love, tough love, courageous love, or divine love.

I think the highest love the Beatles sang about is in alignment with the love Martin Luther King was talking about in the '60s:

"I know that love is ultimately the only answer to mankind's problems. And I'm going to talk about it everywhere I go. I know it isn't popular to talk about it in some circles today. I'm not talking about emotional bosh when I talk about love, I'm talking about a strong, demanding love. And I have seen too much hate…I have decided to love. If you are seeking the highest good, I think you can find it through love. And the beautiful thing is that we are moving against wrong when we do it, because John was right, God is love. He who hates does not know God, but he who has love has the key that unlocks the door to the meaning of ultimate reality."

The New Thought thinker Ernest Holmes invited us to:

"Think for a moment about the few upon whom you have lavished particular affection. Now permit your imagination to include more. Say to yourself: 'What would it be like if these few whome I love so much were multiplied so that finally everyone I meet should arouse in me the same deep affection?' Dare to lose your small affection and you will find it increased and multiplied a million times through greater union."

Perhaps when the Beatles sing "All You Need is Love," what they really mean is all that we need to do is give up anything in our lives that would deny love, and any part of ourselves we view despondently from it?

The Beatles Sixth Commandment

"Don't You Know It's Gonna be Alright"

The Beatles' sixth commandment is a warning not
to give up faith.

The Beatles sixth commandment speaks to
what may seemingly be the most practiced act of
faith of individuals-the belief that everything
is going to be okay.

Have you ever had someone tell you, "Don't
worry, everything is going to be all right?"
Did you believe them? Did you say "How do you
know?" You probably believed them.

This faith seems to be based in the belief
that there is a fundamental good in the cosmos
that transcends opposites, most importantly
good and evil. This idea was well formulated
in the works of Plato and followers of his like

Plotinus. Plotinus, for example, taught that God was good and only good. Like the color white being the embodiment of all color, the whole of life is good when you put the whole wild honey pie together.

He said, "Let us, therefore, re-ascend to the good itself, which every soul desires; and in which it can alone find perfect repose."

Yes, there are polarities in our everyday lives. A yin yang, love and fear, up and down. Yet, is there a good that overcomes all evil like a light that overcomes the darkness? The Beatles song affirms this.

The notion that things work out for the best carries with it faith in retribution, justice, and divine law. Not necessarily because of a God who is like a King, ready to put things aright; because of Divine principle, it is just the way things work. It means that when faced with all of life's so far unanswerable questions—"Will we ever reconnect?" "Will I live on after death?", "Why am I here?", "What the hell is going on here?"—that the answers to all of these questions are ultimately good.

If we cannot accept a view that things tend toward the positive, perhaps we can at least accept that that our view in any given situation is limited. There is more to see, more to know, more to understand. The Beatles are telling us about the view that can contain all, this whole perspective, and that knowledge is indeed available in every piece of our lives.

It is knowledge of the whole of things that helps me to know that even though I am in conflict and feeling separated from someone I love, the truth is I love him and we are connected. It is this knowledge that helps me understand that even in failure, I can learn. That even in grief, there is relief. That "this too shall pass." Why? Because there is, and always will be, more to it than that.

The Beatles' sixth commandment encourages us to trust in a fundamental good in our lives.

The writer Walker Percy asked, "Suppose you ask God for a miracle and God says yes, very well. How do you live the rest of your life?"

How might life be different if we knew without a doubt that a greater good lies over the horizon for all of us? Some might argue we'd feel more free to make mistakes. I'd argue that if we knew our betterment was always ahead, we'd walk more in alignment with it. It would straighten us out. Like Paul does in the song, we can follow the sun, and like George we can say, "it's alright."

The Beatles' Seventh Commandment

"Ob-la-Di Ob-la-Da Life Goes On"

The Beatles' seventh commandment is a warning against missing out on your life.

Could the Beatles' seventh commandment give us insight about life after death? Does life really go on with or without us or like George Harrison put it, "Life goes on within and without us." As the Indian Sage Ramana Maharshi might say, it depends on who is asking the question.

Ob-La-Di Ob-La-Da speaks to the activities of everyday life in their fullness- in the marketplace, being with the children, singing with the band.

The lyrics don't speak to the future or the past, but living ever more so in the "now." They seem to be conveying to us to enjoy life, play with family, be yourself. Could doing these things give us clues about the afterlife? Perhaps when spiritual teachers talk about living in the present moment, they don't generally mean if it is 2:00 p.m. try to live in 2:00 p.m. as long as possible (when would you have dinner?). They are saying living with our awareness as focused on what is here and now as who we are as much as possible gives us the best experience of life. We can begin to cultivate a connection and harmony with everything around us.

This is the meaning behind activities like meditation. One term for where we are in consciousness in these moments is called "The eternal now." John is right, there is no heaven. There is no future. There is only this eternal now. Whether you have a working belief in life after death or lack there-of, the eternal now is helpful to consider if only for the practical consequence that it would help us better to live more in the present as opposed to the dreadfulness of past regrets and future worries.

Whatever you believe about the afterlife-and I would argue we all believe something no matter how much we might attempt to not think about it(we just have less thoughtful guesses is all)-that belief affects you on a daily basis. In that sense it is not really a very metaphysical question at all, for how you live each day, and how you treat others, and what your goals are, are very much influenced by what direction you think you may be headed in. Whether you are living it up to the fullest, or think you'll be back soon, or you're living for heavenly reward, our beliefs about after-life quite simply influence our daily life.

German philosopher Nietzsche theorized what he called the eternal return as an interpretation of life that was never ending yet excluded a "here after." There is life after life, but there is only this life. We reincarnate into the same form, in the same life, at the same time- wherein we do the same things, make the same choices, and pass the same way. Everything is the same, ad infinitum.

As one ponders this understanding, for some of us this may sound like heaven, for others hell. Maybe it is all the same thing over and over but from multiple perspectives? Eventually we might earn a full perspective, and then and only then, life would go on.

The Beatles' Eighth Commandment

"Come Together"

The Beatles' Eighth Commandment is a warning against the foolishness of self-denial.

As touched upon in the discussion of the symbolism of John in the Beatles, "Come Together" is reminiscent of what Carl Jung called "individuation," the coming together of opposites within the individual resulting in harmony.

Have you ever confronted two opposing parts of yourself? Perhaps a part that wanted to be married and another that wanted to be single? Perhaps a part of you that wanted another bowl of ice cream (or two or three), and a part of you that felt violated that you allowed yourself the first?

These are representative of opposing
elements within the self. "Coming Together"
means the two merge to result in wholeness.
Part of coming together is recognizing that
each side has validity based on the perspective
it is coming from. To only listen or heed one
"voice" is to subjugate the other. This
doesn't go away, but festers in the
subconscious. Without mindfulness, without
really listening even if we don't act on its
whims, this voice can act out in us from time
to time, sometimes in unhealthy and destructive
ways.

We find this in John's songs like "Yer
Blues" something quite fascinating, and despite
the lyrics, life affirming. The affirmation of
life comes in that John is, in a sense,
honoring his "shadow side," the part of him
that if he does not "sing his song" will reap
poisonous fruit within.

Acknowledging your shadow side means you listen to it. What it says on the surface may sound disturbing. "I want my husband gone." "I don't want to work anymore." But listen carefully and inquire deeper into "Why?" and you may find that the voice is really saying, "I want independence." We may not want to go through with the initial crying out, but perhaps there is something we can do to increase our liberation, if only to at least feel truly ourselves.

Another way of coming together is through the power of imagery and symbols. This is reflected in the song "Come Together," where common language takes a back seat to "old flattop," and "joo-joo eyeball."

Alchemy was the practice of combining chemicals together to form other chemicals—the most precious being gold. For many, including Carl Jung, alchemy was a metaphor for the psychological process. The gold of the mind

may be wholeness, or freedom, or "true love."
As the song tells us we have to be free.

Joseph Campbell famously said that life is
not a problem to be solved, but a mystery to be
lived. The same is true about ourselves. We
may not "figure ourselves out" or get "to the
root of our problems," but we can be who we are
fully and perhaps even effortlessly. The
qualities we express then—the freedom, the joy,
the presence—this is what we may find to be
what the search was for all along.

The Beatles' Ninth Commandment

"Let It Be"

The Beatles' ninth commandment is a warning against resisting what is.

Let it Be. What a powerful yet simple suggestion. "Let it Be" is the Beatles commandment that gives us the best view of that practice called forgiveness.

We've all heard "let it go," and as good advice as that sometimes is, to let something go is to release it to do something else. To "Let it Be" is to allow "it" to become.

Have you ever had the experience where worrying about an outcome impeded the outcome? Has your paranoia around a relationship, for example, ever contributed to its failure?

To "Let It be" is to suspend judgment in a circumstance. To "Let It Be" is to hold someone to the present and not the past. To "Let It Be" is to hold yourself present and not to the past. To "Let It Be" is to set forth your intention to live in accordance with your values, releasing any attachment to outcome.

There is a spiritual function to "Let It Be." It has to do with truth. It has to do with faith. It has to do with grace.

These are symbolic of the letting down of burdens. Letting them down to be carried by life itself, by the universe, by God, and indeed, to let them carry you too.

The Catholic mystic Meister Eckhardt said, "What is truth? The truth is something so noble, that if God could turn aside from it, I could keep truth and let God go."

In Zen Buddhism they have a saying: "If you see the Buddha, kill him."

No one means turn away from God or Buddha. They mean the God who is not aligned with truth isn't God. They mean that the Buddha you think you see is never the true Buddha because the Buddha is always more than we think we see.

When it comes to our relationships, our work, and our own self-understanding, we can so often crystallize a perspective that ceases to serve us. Clinging to it causes misery and pain. To "let it be" is to release our notions, and allow what really is to be revealed, whatever it is.

The things we try to control most in our lives are often the things we least understand. Maybe it is wiser to let the mystery be the mystery, and allow itself to make itself known? "Let it be" means confronting life's challenges not with denial, but with trust.

Whatever is unsure in your life, just be your best. Just do your best. What it is, let it become.

The Beatles' Tenth Commandment

"And in the End the Love You Take is Equal to the Love you Make"

The Beatles' Tenth Commandment is a warning against not hiding your love away.

Love is a feeling. Love is a way of acting. Love is even a noun in that it is an active Spirit. Love, more than anything else, is an identity; one that includes our greatest independence and uniqueness, but also our connection with everyone.

The greater our sense of identity the greater our experience of love and life; and at some point in life, all the skins are shed, all the characters have parted, and all that remains is love. I hope that's where you'll find me. I hope that's where I'll find you. No difference between us.

The Beatles' final commandment is an evolution of the golden rule. It is an evolution in that includes more than just "others." Do unto others as you would have them do unto you. Do unto yourself as you would do unto others. Do unto others as they are your self. What we do is done unto us.

"And in the End the Love you Take is Equal to the Love you Make" is an ode not to what we've done, but to what we are doing. Not to who we have been, but to who we now choose to be. Love, like all true feeling, can only be felt here and now. No one ever felt love "then," or "later"; one only reaps it now. When we bring consciousness to what we "sow," what we reap makes sense. We can feel it. The trick is to not stop sowing.

The greatest pitfall in life is having a good time and not knowing it. To allow your life and your love to pass you by without your experience of it is tragic. The love we take is the love we are present for and as.

"The End" was the Beatles' last recorded song together. It is fitting because the message of the song is that it doesn't matter that it is. Like any great song, we can play it all over again, but hopefully listen more in tune with its message. The song doesn't have to be "The End"; as Mick Jagger sings on "Shine a Light," we can make any song our favorite tune.

Perhaps the opportunity to listen to a song over and over is one of the most special things about it? We get to understand it a little more each time. Embody it in a way each time. Like in our previous mention of Nietzsche, perhaps our lives are kind of like this too. The times may have past, but the experience is still available, as much as our senses and consciousness are open. If we turn the record to the other side, the flip side is still right there.

We've explored in this work the importance of not finding richness through riches but appreciation. Thinking for ourselves because that's the only medium we have to live in—ourselves. We've talked about living in the now and trusting in the fundamental good, connecting opposites and forgiveness.

When in alignment with these understandings, we understand them more deeply, and hopefully we live each day practicing heightened love for life; love that will cultivate and grow. And when in contact with all the "big life stuff" we struggle to understand, either we will come to understand, or it won't matter much anyhow.

If we get it all, the best thing to do is not to make it harder. Just like a good record, start it over again, get it a little bit more each time, and hopefully get a little stomping

of the feet in the process.